Horse Trivia

by
Diana Benedict

Quinlan Press
Boston

Published by:
Quinlan Press
131 Beverly Street
Boston, MA 02114

ISBN 0-933341-93-8
LC 87-43039

Cover design by Lawrence Curcio

Printed in the United States of America, 1988

Diana Benedict's father taught her how to ride before she entered school. An only child, she grew up with the Arabian horses owned by her parents; today, she and her husband, both educators, also enjoy breeding and raising Arabian horses. A graduate of the University of Washington, Benedict has been a local 4-H leader and supports her three children's efforts with their own horses. She is currently writing another book about her favorite subject.

DEDICATION

This book is lovingly dedicated to the memory of my parents, Merle Benedict and Florence Maddox Benedict.

Contents

Famous Horses and Riders

1.   The most celebrated war horse of all time was owned by Alexander the Great. What was his name?

2.   What color was General Lee's famous mount?

3.   Little Sorrel, or Fancy, was the name of what Confederate general's horse, ridden at Bull Run?

4.   What was the name of the charger ridden by El Cid?

5.   What color was Napoleon's famous Marengo?

Famous Horses and Riders—Questions

6.   What chestnut Thoroughbred did the Duke of Wellington ride at Waterloo?

7.   About what famous horse did Anna Sewell write?

8.   What was the name of the son of the Black Stallion?

9.   What was the name of the colt in Walter Farley's *The Blood Bay Colt?*

10.   Who starred in the movie *International Velvet?*

11.   Who starred in the movie *National Velvet?*

12.   Who played the lead in *The Black Stallion?*

13.   What was the name of the winged steed of Greek mythology?

14.   What was the name of the Lone Ranger's horse?

15.   What did Roy Rogers call his famous horse?

16.   What was the name of the talking horse who had a regular TV show?

17.   What famous Spanish warrior ordered

that his embalmed body be strapped to his mount to ride against the Moors?

18. What was the theme song for Roy Rogers and Dale Evans?

19. What was the name of Tonto's horse?

20. A famous Mounty was St. Preston of the _____.

21. Morzello was the only war horse to be worshipped in a temple with offerings at the foot of his statue. Whose mount had he been?

22. After what city was General Grant's horse named?

23. What black-hatted western hero was played by Bill Boyd?

24. What British cavalryman led the Charge of the Light Brigade on his flashy chestnut Thoroughbred, Ronald?

25. What was the name of the sole survivor of Custer's Last Stand?

26. Who was the Masked Man?

27. Name the "Florence Nightingale of the War Horses" who hunted up British

3

cavalry horses suffering in Cairo and started the Old War Horse Memorial in Cairo, which bears her name today.

28. What Prussian monarch was most notable for his excellence as a cavalry commander?

29. What famous confederate general owned the charger Traveler?

30. Old Drummer lived to be so old he earned an obituary in *The Gentleman's Magazine* in 1753. How old was he?

31. What thirteenth-century leader ravaged the whole of the Middle East with a crew of warriors mounted on shaggy ponies?

32. Granat, the horse ridden by Christine Stuckelberger, is what breed?

33. How did Alexander the Great honor his famous horse?

34. What cowboy star is one of only two actors to appear in *Forbes Magazine*'s annual listing of the four hundred richest people in America?

35. What TV series featured Hoss Cartwright?

36. Who was the most famous Roman chariot

racer, who won 1,462 races beginning in AD 130?

37. Whose stallion was Grane in Wagner's "Ring of the Nibelung"?

38. What famous French jockey is considered by many to be the greatest jockey of all time?

39. What famous jockey, nicknamed "the Shoe," was born in El Paso, Texas, in 1931?

40. In the 1969 movie *The Undefeated*, John Wayne takes three thousand horses originally meant for the Mexican government. What does he do with them?

41. What former steeplechase rider became the turf's best known crime writer?

42. What woman won the dressage competition at the Olympics in 1980 and 1976?

43. What duke was regarded as the greatest horseman of the seventeenth century?

44. What Oglala Sioux leader was named after a horse?

45. Fritz Thiedemann's jumper took part in no fewer than three Olympic games. His name?

46. Frederico Caprilli invented a new style of jumping in 1949. What was it?

47. What was unusual about Stroller winning the silver medal in the Mexican Olympics?

48. What horse did Alwin Schockemole ride to a gold medal in the Montreal Olympics individual event in 1976?

49. What German won the Olympics at Stockholm in 1952 and was World Champion Jumper in 1954 and 1955?

50. Who is the patron saint of farriers?

51. What Charleton Heston movie featured a chariot race?

52. For what is Larry Mahan known?

53. The US won the Olympic team gold for the first time in show jumping in what year?

54. Who stands guard mounted on horseback on Wilshire Boulevard in Beverly Hills?

55. Joe Fargis won the Olympics individual show jumping events on what horse?

56. What nation won the Olympic team show jumping event in 1956, 1960 and 1964?

57. The largest number of horses ever assembled for a film was eight thousand in what US movie?

58. Who won the International Combined Driving Championship in 1977, 1978, 1979, 1980 and 1981?

59. Who wrote "Paul Revere's Ride"?

60. Who rode the drunk horse in *Cat Ballou*?

61. What is the teaching staff at the French National Equestrian Institute called?

62. What was the highest earning western?

63. What Greek mythological figure was half god and half man?

64. In *Love's Labours Lost*, Shakespeare refers to a horse that "danced" before crowded galleries in the courtyard of an inn on Ludgate Hill. What was the horse's name?

65. Who directed *Blazing Saddles*?

66. In 1962, who starred as Lawrence in *Lawrence of Arabia*?

67. Why does Marilyn Monroe oppose Clark Gable's roping horses in *The Misfits*?

68.   What famous female sharpshooter made her film debut in 1894?

69.   What famous western author write the first feature-length color western, premiered in 1924?

70.   What cowboy star of silent westerns is commemorated with a statue of a riderless pony at the spot in Arizona where he died in a car crash?

71.   What prophet said,
        "Blessed be ye, O Daughters of the wind?"

72.   Who was the "Electric Horseman"?

73.   Who was "Bronco Billy"?

74.   Who was voted the most popular Western star each year from 1936 to 1942?

75.   Who was voted the most popular Western star each year from 1943 to 1954?

76.   What Western hero has been most often portrayed on the screen?

77.   What fifties star got a record $750,000 salary for his part in *The Horse Soldiers*?

78.   What trick rider was the first professional Hollywood stuntwoman and doubled for

Helen Holmes in the "Hazards of Helen" episodes (1914)?

79. In 1969 John Wayne won his Oscar as a boozing, aging lawman in what western?

80. What famous woman is commemorated by a statue of her astride her magnificent horse in the city of Paris?

81. What was the name of Bill Steinkraus's mount in 1968 when he won the individual gold at the Mexican Olympics?

82. Who was captain of the US Olympic team in 1956?

83. Halla is the courageous little mare from Germany who won the individual gold and the team gold. Who was her rider?

84. David Broome won his World Championship riding a very difficult horse who shared the name of a musical composer. What was the horse's name?

85. What brilliant Brazilian rider won the gigantic Hamburg Derby on four occasions riding Gran Geste?

86. What famous member of royalty rode Doublet in three Day Events?

87. What famous horse, owned by Paul

Mellon, won in 1971 the Eclipse Stakes, the English Derby, the Prix do l'Arc de Triomphe, and the King George VI and Queen Elizabeth Stakes?

88. The great Nijinsky was bred in Canada. In what country was he trained?

89. Two famous Crillo ponies, Mancha and Gato, were ridden thirteen thousand miles in 1920 to prove their stamina. The ride took two and a half years and went from Buenos Aires to what American city?

90. King Solomon was an authority on what horsebreed?

91. What breed are these famous American horses: Stonewall, Bourbon, Anacacho, Peavine, Kalarama and Wing Commander?

92. What Polish imported Arabian was the greatest influence on American breeding, winning National Champion three times (in hand, under saddle and in harness)?

93. A movie has been made about the life of this famous Australian racehorse, with his name as the title. Bred in New Zealand in 1926, he died in California in 1932. His name?

94. What events won fame for the horse

Salad Days: rodeo, racing, Olympics, vaulting or halter futurity?

95. Van Dyck's famous painting *Charles I on Horseback* depicts Charles on what color of mount?

96. Who painted *The Polish Horseman*?

97. What breed are these famous horses: Adios, The Widower, Good Time, Gene Abbe, Nevele Pride and Bret Hanover?

98. What famous Arab stallion, when mated with his own daughter, sired the legendary *Raffles?

99. Who was the foundation sire of the King Ranch in Kingsville, Texas?

100. What breed has these famous horses in its registry: Joe Cody, Cutter Bill and What a Bonanza?

101. What famous Arabian farm owned and stood *Bask?

102. What famous sport horse, a Trakehner, is being syndicated into one hundred shares valued at $35,000 each?

103. What famous jockey, now a paraplegic, rode Secretariat to his 1973 Triple Crown victories?

Answers

1.   Bucephalus

2.   Confederate gray

3.   Thomas J. "Stonewall" Jackson

4.   Babieca

5.   Grey or white

6.   Copenhagen

7.   Black Beauty

8.   Satan

9.   Bonfire

Famous Horses and Riders—Answers

10.   Tatum O'Neal

11.   Elizabeth Taylor

12.   Kelly Reno

13.   Pegasus

14.   Silver

15.   Trigger

16.   Mr. Ed

17.   El Cid

18.   "Happy Trails"

19.   Scout

20.   Yukon

21.   Cortez's

22.   Cincinnati

23.   Hopalong Cassidy

24.   Lord Cardigan

25.   A buckskin named Comanche. He had
        twelve wounds and spent a year in slings
        before becoming fully recovered. Cavalry

headquarters allowed him complete freedom for the rest of his life at Fort Riley, Kansas.

26. The Lone Ranger

27. Dorothy Brooke

28. Frederick the Great

29. General Robert E. Lee

30. Forty-five

31. Genghis Khan

32. Holstein

33. He named a Greek town after him.

34. Gene Autry

35. "Bonanza"

36. Diocles

37. Brunhilde's

38. Yves St. Martin

39. Willie Shoemaker

40. He delivers them to the rebel forces.

Famous Horses and Riders—Answers

41. Dick Francis

42. Christine Stuckelberger, from Switzerland, on Granat

43. The Duke of Newcastle, William Cavendish

44. Chief Crazy Horse

45. Meteor

46. Leaning forward rather than backwards during a jump

47. His size: he is a pony.

48. Warwick Rex

49. Hans Gunter Winkler

50. St. Eligius

51. *Ben Hur*

52. Winning rodeo events

53. 1984

54. John Wayne

55. Touch of Class

16

Famous Horses and Riders—Answers

56. Germany

57. *War and Peace*

58. Gregory Bardos of Hungary

59. Henry Wadsworth Longfellow

60. Lee Marvin

61. *Cadre Noir*

62. *Butch Cassidy and the Sundance Kid*

63. The centaur

64. Morocco

65. Mel Brooks

66. Peter O'Toole

67. The horses will be used for dogfood.

68. Annie Oakley

69. Zane Grey

70. Tom Mix

71. Mohammed

72. Robert Redford

73. The first western star, G.M. Anderson, who made nearly four hundred Bronco Billy pictures

74. Gene Autry

75. Roy Rogers

76. William F. "Buffalo Bill" Cody — in forty-seven films or more

77. Both John Wayne and William Holden

78. Helen Gibson, wife of cowboy star Hoot Gibson

79. *True Grit*

80. Joan of Arc

81. Snowbound

82. Bill Steinkraus

83. Hans Winkler

84. Beethoven

85. Nelson Pessoa

86. Princess Anne

87. Mill Reef

Famous Horses and Riders—Answers

88. Ireland

89. New York

90. Arabian

91. Saddlebred

92. Bask

93. Phar Lap

94. Olympics

95. Gray

96. Rembrandt

97. Standardbred

98. Skowronek

99. Old Sorrel

100. American Quarter Horse Association

101. Lasma

102. Abdullah

103. Ron Turcotte

Lingo

1. Herring gutted means a horse is slack and undeveloped through the _____.

2. What are people referring to when they say a horse carries a good flag?

3. Good clean bone refers to which bone?

4. A good post horse is quiet and mannerly where?

5. What do you call a canter in Western talk?

6. What name is given to a golden horse with a flaxen mane and tail?

7. What is a baby female horse called?

8. What is a dam of a foal?

9. What marking is a patch of white in the middle of the forehead?

10. What is a cob?

11. What is meconium?

12. A wide band of white from the forehead to the nose is called a _____.

13. What is the name given to the antibody-rich first milk of a mare?

14. What is the result of a zebra and a horse interbreeding?

15. A narrow band of white from the forehead to the nose is a _____.

16. A snip is a small patch of white near the _____.

17. What do you call a horse with a yellow coat, and a black mane and tail with black stockings?

18. A buckskin of bluish or lavender color with black points and an eel stripe is called what?

19. What do you call a springy trot performed without any forward movement?

20. A Lipizzan rider would call a turn on the haunches a _____.

21. What is a nick to a breeder?

22. True or False: A horse's crest is on top of his head.

23. If a horse is balancing perfectly still on its hind legs, it is performing what move?

24. A Paso Fino doing a true pace at full speed is doing the _____.

25. A Paint or Pinto may have his marking described by which two terms?

26. What is the name of the vehicle pulled by a harness racer?

27. What is a horse that swallows air called?

28. What word is used to describe oscillating motions while standing in one place, characterized by stabled horses?

29. What is bloom?

30. A breeder is defined as the owner of the _____ at the time of service.

31. What are calked shoes?

32. A horse that is cat-hammed is poorly muscled in the _____.

33. What is a defect called that was acquired during development within the uterus?

34. What is a colt?

35. What is a cryptorchid?

36. What is the sire of a foal?

37. What does a farrier do?

38. What do you call a female horse under four that has never had a foal?

39. What is flushing?

40. What are get?

41. How many inches equal one hand?

42. What kind of blood does a hot-blooded horse have?

43. What do you call a slow trot?

44. What do you call a three-year-old horse that has produced a foal?

45. What do you do when you mount?

46. What is parturition?

47.   Regardless of the genes it possesses, the visible characteristics of an animal are called its _____.

48.   What is prepotency?

49.   To what does "at liberty" refer?

50.   What is the literal translation of the word dressage?

51.   What is a volte?

52.   When the horse changes leads in the air in one stride, what is it called?

53.   Two voltes with a change of hand constitute what maneuver?

54.   What is meant by the inside leg?

55.   What is the active leg of the rider?

56.   What is a rejoneador?

57.   What do you call the horse that runs alongside the bull, keeping it accessible to the bulldogger?

58.   What is the original meaning of the words *caballero* and *chevalier*?

59.   What is a disunited horse?

60. What do you say to make a horse stop?

61. Who is the M.F.H. to hunt fans?

62. Define hot walker.

63. What do you call the part of the horse in front of the rider?

64. What does the drag do on a trail ride?

65. What is another name of supernumerary premolars?

66. Mongolians drink kumiss. What is it?

67. Where does the term stallion originate?

68. According to international ruling, every horse with a withers height less than 148 centimeters is considered to be a
_____.

69. True or False: Cold-blooded horses have a lower body temperature than warm-blooded breeds.

70. What is the tolt?

71. What is the flehmen response?

72. What sport are these terms from: flag, mill, flank-vault and scissors?

73. What is the Argentinian game on horseback similar to basketball called?

74. What is a *jineteada*?

75. What is the first part of a driving event called?

76. What is the bottom side of a pedigree?

77. What do you call the area of a horse's back behind the saddle?

78. What riding seat was evolved from the seat used by plantation horses in the South?

79. What Anglo-Saxon word means "a field day on horseback"?

80. What is fuzztail running?

81. What is a green horse?

82. What do you call a tight, fast, 180-degree turn at speed on horseback?

83. What is the web of the horseshoe?

84. An Arab of this color is called chestnut. What word is used for a quarter horse of this color?

85.   What word is used for a horse that has patches of white on a coat color other than black: piebald or skewbald?

86.   What was the job of the costermonger's pony?

87.   What is a pipe-opener?

88.   Where are a horse's feathers?

89.   What is riding pillion?

90.   What color is the iris of a walleyed horse?

91.   What is the term used to describe a neck that shows a distinct depression in front of the withers?

92.   What is a quittor?

93.   What is a free-legged pacer?

94.   Describe a hunter clip.

95.   What is over-reaching?

96.   What is "hogging" the mane?

97.   What is the U.S.E.T.?

98.   What is the F.E.I.?

Answers

1.   loins

2.   The set of the tail

3.   The canon

4.   In the starting gate

5.   A lope

6.   Palomino

7.   A filly

8.   Its mother

9.   A star

Lingo—Answers

10. A large pony of the riding and driving type

11. The foal's first fecal movement

12. blaze

13. Colostrum

14. A zebrorse

15. stripe or strip

16. nostril

17. A dun or buckskin

18. A grullo, grulla, mouse dun or coyote dun

19. A piaffe

20. passade

21. A cross that consistently produces champions

22. False

23. The levade

24. andadura

25. Overo or tobiano

Lingo—Answers

26.   A sulky

27.   A cribber or windsucker

28.   Weaving

29.   Hair that is very healthy, clean and shiny

30.   mare

31.   Shoes having projections downward from the toe or heel to provide better traction

32.   hindquarters

33.   Congenital

34.   A young male horse (usually under four)

35.   A stallion with one or both testicles retained in the abdominal cavity

36.   Its father

37.   Trim horses' hooves and shoe them

38.   A filly

39.   Feeding a thin mare more heavily prior to breeding in order to increase fertility

40.   Offspring of a stallion

Lingo—Answers

41. Four

42. Eastern or oriental blood

43. A jog

44. A mare

45. Get on the horse

46. The act of giving birth

47. phenotype

48. The ability of an animal to pass its characteristics on to its offspring

49. Showing a horse without any restraints

50. Training

51. A turn on a small circle

52. A flying lead change

53. A figure of eight

54. The leg of the rider or horse that is towards the center when working in a circle

55. The leg being used to command the horse

56. A mounted Torero

Lingo—Answers

57. The header

58. Horseman

59. A horse that travels on one lead in front and an opposite lead behind

60. "Whoa"

61. The Master of Fox Hounds

62. A mechanical device used for conditioning horses

63. Forehand

64. He rides the trail after the riders to help out in emergencies.

65. Wolf teeth

66. Fermented mare's milk

67. "Stalled one" or one kept in a stable

68. pony

69. False

70. A gait between a normal walk and a pace, very comfortable to the rider.

71. Lifting the head and curling back the upper lip

72. Circus gymnastics or gymnastics on horseback

73. *El pato*

74. A rodeo in South America

75. Presentation

76. The dam's side

77. The croup

78. Saddleseat

79. *Gymkhana*

80. Catching wild horses

81. An inexperienced or broken but not fully trained horse

82. A rollback

83. Measurement of width

84. Sorrel

85. Skewbald

86. To pull a cart of fruit, fish, vegetables, etc.

87. A sharp exercise burst at a fast speed

88. On his lower legs

89. Sitting sideways on a horse

90. Pearly white

91. Ewe-necked or set-on upside down

92. A festering sore anywhere along the border of the coronet or the top of the hoof wall

93. A pacer that races without hobbles

94. The body is fully clipped but long hair is left on the legs for protection.

95. The heels of the forefeet get hit by the toes of the hind feet.

96. Cutting the hair right back to the neckline

97. The United States Equestrian Team

98. The Federation of Equestre Internationale

Breeds

1. What country first recognized and improved breeding of the Paso Fino?

2. In 1965 the first Peruvian Pasos came to what state in the US?

3. The running walk was made famous by what breed?

4. To what does the punch of the Suffolk Punch refer?

5. Viking ships brought what kind of ponies to the Shetland Islands two thousand years ago?

6. What breed are the following famous

horses: Toi Soldier, Mi Toska, Ga'zi, El Hilal, Ferda and Scarlet Lace?

7. Both George Washington and Thomas Jefferson owned horses of which breed?

8. The Barb originated where?

9. All Thoroughbreds trace directly to what three horses?

10. All Thoroughbreds have their birthday on what day?

11. Can a horse be registered in more than one breed registry?

12. Thoroughbreds are registered with what breed organization?

13. A Thoroughbred's name must not include more than _____ letters.

14. The Morgan breed stems from a single bay stallion. His name?

15. What two states produced the first American saddle horses?

16. What Saddlebred won the Grand Champion Five Gaited Stake in Kentucky for six successive years?

17. Rysdsyk's Hambletonian was a foundation sire of what breed?

18. The official sire of the American Saddlebred is a race horse named _____.

19. The fast, artificial three-beat gait of the Saddlebred is called the _____.

20. The Appaloosa horse was bred by what Indian tribe?

21. True or False: Arabs traced a horse's descent through the dam's side.

22. From what country is the Lipizzan breed?

23. Appaloosa horses originally took their name from what river?

24. In 1870 an estimated ninety percent of the horses used for pulling carriages, streetcars and coaches in America were what breed?

25. What does *paso fino* mean in Spanish?

26. What does A.Q.H.A. stand for?

27. The foundation sire of the Standardbred breed was a grey thoroughbred called _____.

28. The Chincoteague Islands are off the coat of which state?

29. What breed of horse was Mr. Ed?

30. What breed of horse could run a quarter of a mile faster than any other in 1690?

31. What does POA stand for?

32. Belgians and Clydesdales both evolved from what mighty war horse of the middle ages?

33. What breed of horse is *always* bay with black mane, tail and lower legs?

34. The Clydesdale originated in Scotland near what river?

35. What breed was the most popular draft horse at the beginning of this century?

36. Which breed of draft horse is the tallest?

37. What breed of horse starred in the movie *The Black Stallion*?

38. Which breed is taller, the Mustang or the Percheron?

39. To what horse can every Suffolk Punch trace back?

40. The Percheron is most often what color?

41. Which is the shortest draft horse breed?

42. What are the shires of Britain?

43. What draft breed is only allowed to be chestnut in color?

44. What breed is called the "large black old English horse"?

45. What Quarter Horse mare was Reserve World Champion Cutting horse five times and N.C.H.A. World Championship Cutting Horse Mare three times?

46. As early as 1493, who brought good breeding stock to the colony at Santo Domingo?

47. In Claremore, Oklahoma, there is a statue of Will Rogers on what breed of horse?

48. What famous sire of quarter runners was imported by Mordecai Booth in the 1850s?

49. What does a star in front of an Arab's name signify?

50. What two breeds are combined for the National Show Horse Registry?

51. What color was the important Quarter Horse sire Steel Dust?

52. In what year was the American Quarter Horse Association formed?

53. True or False: Hunter is a breed of horse.

54. What two breeds are combined in the Anglo-Arab?

55. The Criollo is a small, hardy breed from what continent?

56. Who got the honorific number one in the first stud book of the A.Q.H.A.?

57. A Paint horse is always one of which two breed registries?

58. What does ROM mean to quarter horse point competitors?

59. The Trakehner breed originated at the Trakehnen Stud in what country?

60. The Waler is a modern saddle horse from what country?

61. True or False: Paint and Pinto are the same thing.

62. What breed is divided into these three types: Kuhaylan, Saqlawi and Munigi?

63.   In the Civil War, which breed of horse was most often used by the Northerners?

64.   What color should the skin of an Arab be?

65.   What is distinctive about the Falabella pony?

66.   True or False: It only costs one-third to one-fifth as much to keep a pony as it does a horse.

67.   What happens to the surplus young stallions of Assateague?

68.   True or False: About half of the million horses in Yugoslavia are Bosnian ponies.

69.   Galiceno ponies come from what country?

70.   What does POA stand for?

71.   These characteristics are of what breed: pink pigment around the eyes, nose and under the tail, with striated hooves?

72.   What breed name is said to have come from the Castilian word *mesteno*?

73.   Henry VIII rudely likened his Queen Anne of Cleves to what breed of mare?

74. In what country were Trakehners and Hanoverians bred?

75. Where was the famous Arab sire Skowrenek born?

76. Lipizzaners actually originated in the Karst region of northern _____ at the Lipizza stud in the sixteenth century.

77. What state produced the Fox Trotting Horse?

78. What is an Arab's jibbah?

79. What is the name of the arch in an Arab's neck at the top of the crest?

80. What wild horse of Russia and Eastern Europe has been reconstituted in Poland?

81. What is the oldest pure breed in the world?

82. Saddlebreds have their dock muscles nicked and their tail set in a _____.

83. The Standardbred originated two hundred years ago in what country?

84. Where did the term Standardbred come from?

Breeds—Questions

85.   What is the peculiar gait of the Missouri Fox Trotter?

86.   What breed was formerly known as the Turn-Row because it could travel between rows of crops without damaging them?

87.   What country boasts the breeds called the Brumb and the Waler?

88.   The US can claim it is the country of origin of only *one* breed of draft horse. Which?

89.   What term for an offspring of a Thoroughbred mare bred to a Percheron stallion called Pete Larex has been patented?

90.   The Avelignese pony of Italy is always what color?

91.   Where is the Basuto pony found?

92.   What color is an albino horse's eyes?

93.   The wild Camargue pony of southeastern France is what color?

94.   For what is the tiny Falabella pony of Argentina named?

95.   Orlovs are trotting horses from where?

96. What country do these pony breeds come from: Fell, Dales, Exmoor, New Forest and Dartmoor?

97. What are the six basic coat patterns used to describe Appaloosas?

98. Who was the POA's foundation sire, bred in 1956 by Leslie Boomhower of Mason City, Iowa?

99. How tall is the Soviet Budeonny: thirteen, fourteen, fifteen or sixteen hands?

100. What two breeds were crossed to produce the POA's foundation sire?

101. The island of Timor boasts a pony breed also named Timor. Where is the island of Timor?

102. What Danish breed of spotted horse dates back to the Napoleonic Wars?

103. Kladrubers from Czechoslovakia were developed as coach and parade horses for the imperial court in Vienna. By the nineteenth century, all but two colors had been bred out. Which two?

104. Russian Trotters are a combination of Orlovs and what American breed?

105. Homer Davenport wrote *My Quest of the _____ Horse*.

106. Where is the British annual Thoroughbred Stallion Show held each year?

107. On the female side, the Arabian foundation mare called _____ was the pervading influence in early Thoroughbred breeding.

108. In 1949 an Act of Parliament was passed that changed the appearance of the Welsh cobs. What did the act prohibit?

109. No other country in the world breeds such a great variety of ponies as _____.

110. What great gray Standardbred gelding in 1938 set a new record time of 1.55¼. He was named after a breed of dog.

111. Where is the famous Janow Podlaksi stud?

112. What spotted horse breed from Denmark is very popular for circus work?

113. True or False: No native ponies were available on Iceland when the Norse settled that island.

114. What are the Brumby?

115. Black Allen sired Roan Allen, Hunter's Allan and Merry Legs. These are the foundations of what breed?

116. The Morgan horse, later named Justin Morgan, was originally called _____.

117. What three American breeds has the Morgan greatly influenced?

118. What breed did the Moors develop during their eighth-century stay in Al Andalus, Spain?

119. What country do these pony breeds come from: Panje, Imud, Zeimatuka, Klepper, Bashkir and Viatka?

120. What mare was brought to the World's Columbian Exposition in Chicago in 1893 by some Syrian rug merchants and was purchased by an American, getting the first registration number in the stud book?

121. What did they call Saddlebreds in 1967?

122. Whose most important sons were Sherman, Woodbury, Bulrush and Revenge?

123. What name is given to the product of a Morgan and Arab cross?

Answers

1. Puerto Rico

2. Arizona

3. Tennessee Walker

4. The punched up belly or paunch

5. Shetland Ponies

6. Arabian

7. Thoroughbred

8. The Barbery Coast of North Africa

9. The Godolphin Arabian, the Byerly Tuck and the Darley Arabian

10.   January 1

11.   Yes; for example, Paint and Quarter Horse

12.   The Jockey Club

13.   Sixteen

14.   Justin Morgan or Figure

15.   Kentucky and Tennessee

16.   Wing Commander

17.   Standardbred

18.   Denmark

19.   rack

20.   Nez Perce

21.   True

22.   Austria

23.   The Palouse

24.   Morgan

25.   Fine step

26.   American Quarter Horse Association

27. Messenger

28. Virginia

29. Palomino

30. Quarter Horse

31. Pony of the Americas

32. The Horse of Flanders

33. Cleveland Bay

34. Clyde

35. Percheron

36. Shire

37. Arabian

38. Percheron

39. The Crisp Horse

40. Gray or black

41. Suffolk Punch

42. Counties

43. Suffolk Punch

44. Shire

45. Poco Lena

46. Christopher Columbus

47. Quarter Horse

48. Janus

49. Importation

50. Arabian and Saddlebred

51. Bay

52. 1940

53. False

54. Arabian and Thoroughbred

55. South America

56. Wimpy

57. Quarter Horse or Thoroughbred

58. Register of Merit

59. Prussia

60. Australia

61. False

62. The Arabian

63. The Morgan

64. Black

65. Their size; they are too small even to be ridden by children.

66. True

67. They are made to swim across the channel to Chincoteague and sold at public auction.

68. True

69. Mexico

70. Pony of the Americas

71. Appaloosa

72. Mustang

73. Flanders or Belgium

74. Germany

75. Poland

Breeds—Answers

76. Yugoslavia

77. Missouri

78. The broad, bulging forehead

79. Mitbah

80. The Tarpan

81. The Arab

82. crupper

83. America

84. From the time standard, which was adopted to test the ability of harness racers before admitting them to the American Trotter Register

85. It walks with forefeet and trots with hind feet.

86. Tennessee Walker

87. Australia

88. Cream Draft

89. Thorcheron

90. Chestnut

Breeds—Answers

91.   Africa

92.   Blue

93.   Gray

94.   The family that developed the breed in Buenos Aires

95.   Russia

96.   England

97.   Frost, leopard, marble, snowflake, spotted blanket and white blanket

98.   Black Hand

99.   Sixteen hands

100. Shetland and Appaloosa

101. Indonesia

102. Knabstrup

103. Black and white

104. Standardbreds

105. Arabian

106. Newmarket

107. Old Bald Peg

108. Nicking and docking of tails

109. England

110. Greyhound

111. Poland

112. Knabstrup

113. True

114. The wild horses of Australia

115. Tennessee Walker

116. Figure

117. Standardbred, Saddlebred and Tennessee Walking Horse

118. Andalusian

119. U.S.S.R.

120. Nejdme

121. American Saddle Horses

122. Justin Morgan's

123. Morab

Health

1. What is a bony enlargement of the pastern just above the hoof called?

2. Bog spavin is a puffy swelling on the inside and slightly to the front of which joint?

3. When a horse stands back on his heels due to inflammation of the wall of the hoof, he has _____.

4. Shoe boil is another name for what condition?

5. Approximately how many months is a horse's gestation?

6. What is the first shot generally given to all

foals which is also given once yearly for their lifetime?

7.   What is another name for ascarids?

8.   How many gallons of saliva does a horse produce daily?

9.   What insect is a vector for equine infectious anemia?

10.   What is the proper name for Monday-morning sickness?

11.   What are thumps?

12.   A horse should be reshod how often?

13.   Bots are the larvae of what insect?

14.   What internal parasite may be present in a horse that rubs his tail?

15.   What is another name for contagious abortion?

16.   What kind of worms can lead to death from bloodclots?

17.   At what age do foals usually first get wormed?

18.   What is a bolus?

19.   Is it safe to worm a pregnant mare?

20.   What is V.E.E.?

21.   What is another name for distemper in horses?

22.   What is the procedure called where the veterinarian pours liquid wormer directly down the esophagus to the horse's stomach?

23.   What is another word for lockjaw?

24.   Foals usually begin their vaccination programs at what age?

25.   True or False: A horse's body temperature is higher than a human's body temperature.

26.   What is a normal horse's pulse rate?

27.   A normal horse will pass how many pounds of fecal material during a twenty-four hour period?

28.   Why do some horsemen put stones in the grain feedbox?

29.   The average horse urinates eight or nine times a day. How much urine is released each time?

30. Can horses vomit?

31. What is indigestion in a horse called?

32. Where is an intradermal shot given?

33. What is another name for proud flesh?

34. What color of horse is most likely to get a melanoma?

35. Where is an intravenous shot given?

36. Where are tumors most frequently found on horses?

37. What is another word for founder?

38. Moldy hay can cause difficulty in breathing. What is this condition called?

39. True or False: Feed a horse with scours a richer diet.

40. What is a bacterial infection of the mammary tissue of the udder called?

41. Thrush is a disease of what part of the horse?

42. Where is vitamin D synthesized?

43. About how much water will a horse drink during a normal day?

44. Carotene comes from green pasture. It provides what vitamin?

45. What is a drench?

46. When should horses not be given free choice of water?

47. What vitamin increases conception rates and quality of semen?

48. Is it better for a horse to have more calcium or more phosphorous?

49. What is TDN?

50. Should alfalfa be fed free choice?

51. What is the preferred grain to feed horses?

52. When does foal heat generally occur?

53. Pointing indicates what condition?

54. Where is a quarter crack?

55. What might be a problem in a horse that suddenly stops chewing, partly opens his mouth, and shakes his head from side to side?

56. How are horses' teeth floated?

57. True or False: A horse's sense of hearing is very acute.

58. Why would you take cinnamon oil on the road to a horseshow?

59. Where are a horse's chestnuts?

60. At what age do a horse's first permanent teeth erupt?

61. If a horse's upper jaw is overdeveloped and extends beyond the lower jaw, the horse is said to be _____.

62. Which of these plants are poisonous to horses: choke cherry, dandelions, bracken fern or horsetail?

63. True or False: Although some animals have larger eyes in comparison to their body sizes, no land animal has so large an eye as a horse in actual dimensions.

64. When do foals start to lose their baby teeth?

65. True or False: A horse can see straight backward and straight forward at the same time, without moving the head or eye.

66. True or False: The Blackfoot Indians had horse medicine men who were paid to make horses well.

67. Where does the process of fermentation occur in a horse's internal organs?

68. What is an endoscope used to examine?

69. How many months will it take a foal to develop an immune system if he does not receive colostrum?

70. Which horse needs the highest percentage of protein in its feed: a foal, a weanling, a yearling or a mature horse?

71. Why would you tap a horse's forehead?

72. What do the letters L.F.G. in a stallion advertisement mean?

73. What vitamin do mares need especially in the last trimester of their pregnancy?

74. What is used to disinfect the umbilical cord of a newborn foal?

75. Why would you press on the gum of a horse's mouth?

76. What does the assistant hold while the veterinarian floats the teeth?

77. Where does the vet put the tube when he tube worms a horse?

78.   Why would you make a horse with colic walk?

79.   A horse's stomach can hold how many quarts of food?

80.   How many vertebrae do most horse breeds have?

81.   What bones on either side of the cannon bones are remnants of the digits lost during evolution?

82.   How many teeth does an adult horse have?

83.   True or False: The brain of a horse is very large in relation to his size.

84.   True or False: Horses' teeth should be brushed once weekly.

85.   True or False: Eating unmelted snow robs the body of more heat and moisture than can be offset by the amount consumed.

86.   Where are scratches found on a horse?

87.   Where is rain scald found?

88.   How many days can a horse last without water?

Health—Questions

89. What was the single leading cause of serious rider injury in 110 consecutive riding accidents?

90. True or False: The mare is the only animal that fails to provide her baby with antibodies during gestation.

91. What hormone is given to mares who have difficulty passing the placenta?

92. Which has more protein: Kentucky bluegrass or orchardgrass?

93. Heaves refer to an abnormal pattern of _____.

94. How many splint bones does every horse have?

95. Where are heaves lines found?

96. If a sizeable contaminated wound is discovered, do you give the antibiotic before or after cleansing it?

97. What is acetylpromazine used for?

98. What is the proper name for swamp fever?

99. What part of the horse's body provides a full 90 percent of his balance?

65

100. True or False: Granulated tissue is full of exposed nerve endings.

101. What is lordosis?

102. Metritis is the infection of what?

103. Lengthening daylight hours trigger a mare to produce F.S.H. What is it?

104. Does ovulation occur at the beginning or end of estrus?

105. C.I.D. was first recognized in 1973 by researchers at what state university?

106. What is the most common infection to which C.I.D. foals succumb?

107. How many hours a day does a horse sleep?

108. When do horses sleep more: summer or winter?

109. True or False: Seedy toe is caused from horses standing in their grain boxes.

110. True or False: A horse cannot get needed REM sleep without lying down.

111. What kind of pests do these words refer to: blow, deer, screwworm, horn and face?

112. What is the most common fracture to occur in racing?

113. Which has a higher percentage of calcium: alfalfa hay or timothy hay?

114. Why is Lasix (furosemide) given to some racehorses?

115. True or False: Ponies get laminitis more often than other breeds.

116. What bad habit would Forssell's operation prevent?

117. What is the curium?

118. Which is wider, the horse's upper or lower jaw?

119. How long would it take for a horse's hoof to grow from the coronary band at the toe to the ground?

120. True or False: Navicular disease is most commonly found in the hind legs.

121. What condition would cause the farrier to use iodine on your horse's cleft?

122. More lameness in the forelimb occurs in the foot, but where is the weak spot in the hind legs?

123. If a horse has ears that are always moving and picks its feet up high, what health problem could be indicated?

124. Galvayne's groove is a depression found in horses at ten years. Where is it?

125. Which is cause for concern: a horse resting on his foreleg or his hind leg?

126. How old is a horse past mark of mouth?

127. About how much does a horse's heart weigh?

128. If a horse's chest wall is perforated on one side, will both lungs collapse?

129. What is another name for the end bone of the leg, the pedal bone?

130. True or False: A horse's digestive process takes three or four days.

131. Few hunters of worth have less than eight inches of bone. What bone are they talking about?

132. When a person is stifled he is repressed or held back. What does it mean when a horse it stifled?

133. At what month of pregnancy is the sex of the fetus recognizable?

134. True or False: The hind foot of a horse is more pointed at the toe and the sole is more concave than the forefoot.

135. What grain is most commonly fed to horses?

136. Where is the hoof wall the thickest: toe, quarter or heel?

137. When the horse is moving, no matter what the gait, which part of the foot hits the ground first?

138. Why is it unhealthy to sand the outside of the hoof wall?

139. What is C.E.M.?

140. What is dioestrus?

Answers

1. Ringbone

2. Hock

3. laminitis

4. Capped elbow

5. Eleven months

6. Tetanus

7. Large roundworms

8. Ten gallons

9. The mosquito

10.   Azoturia

11.   Hiccups

12.   Every six to eight weeks

13.   The botfly

14.   Pinworms

15.   Rhinopneumonitis

16.   Strongles or bloodworms

17.   Two months

18.   A large pill

19.   Yes

20.   Venezuelan Equine Encephalomyelitis

21.   Strangles

22.   Tube worming

23.   Tetanus

24.   Two to three months

25.   True

26.   Between 35 and 55 beats per minute

27.   Thirty-five to forty pounds

28.   To get the horse to eat more slowly so he won't bolt food or choke

29.   One quart

30.   No

31.   Colic

32.   Into the skin

33.   Granulated tissue

34.   Gray

35.   Into the vein

36.   Under the tail, in the dock area

37.   Laminitis

38.   Pulmonary emphysema, heaves or broken wind

39.   False

40.   Mastitis

41.   The frog of the foot

42.   In the caecum

Health—Answers

43.   Eight to ten gallons

44.   A

45.   A liquid medicine given orally

46.   When overheated

47.   E

48.   Calcium

49.   Total Digestible Nutrient

50.   No

51.   Oats

52.   Nine days after foaling

53.   Lameness

54.   In the half of the hoof nearest the heel

55.   Toothache

56.   The sharp edges are removed with a rasp.

57.   True

58.   To flavor unpalatable drinking water for your horse

59. On his legs

60. Two and a half years

61. parrot-mouthed

62. All but dandelions

63. True

64. At two and a half years

65. True

66. True

67. Large intestine — caecum and large and small colon

68. The mare's uterine lining

69. At least three months

70. A foal

71. To soothe and distract him

72. Live Foal Guarantee

73. Vitamin A, or carotene

74. Iodine

75. To check the capillary refill time by watching the color change from white back to pink

76. The tongue

77. Up one nostril

78. To prevent him from rolling around and twisting his gut

79. Eighteen

80. Twenty-four (Arabs have twenty-three)

81. The splint bone

82. Forty

83. False

84. False

85. True

86. On the back of the pastern, between the fetlock and the coronary band

87. On the horse's back or rump

88. Three

89. Failure to wear safety headgear

90. True

91. Oxytocin

92. Orchardgrass

93. breathing

94. Eight (two on each leg)

95. Behind the ribs along the abdomen (the muscles thicken due to repeated use in exhaling)

96. Before

97. Tranquilizing

98. Infectious anemia

99. The head

100. False

101. Excessive swayback or curvature of the spine

102. The uterus

103. Follicle Stimulating Hormone

104. End

105. Washington State

106. Pneumonia

107. Two and a half to three hours

108. Summer

109. False

110. True. Horses can sleep standing up, but they only get slow-wave sleep benefits.

111. Fly

112. Fracture of the sesamoid bones

113. Alfalfa

114. To prevent bleeding

115. True

116. Cribbing

117. The sensitive tissue layer in the hoof, from which the hoof grows

118. The upper jaw: this enables the sideways grinding motion

119. One year at the toe, about six months at the heel

120. False

121. Thrush

122. In the hock

123. Blindness or visual difficulties

124. In the middle of the tooth on the outer surface of the upper corners

125. Foreleg

126. Over eight

127. Nine pounds

128. Yes

129. Coffin bone or third phalanx

130. True

131. Cannon bone

132. The stifle joint becomes dislocated.

133. At the end of the second month

134. True

135. Oats

136. Toe

137. The heel

138. The sanding removes the natural shiny coating which helps prevent evaporation, thus the hoof will dry out.

139. Contagious equine metritis

140. The fifteen-day period where there is no estrus

Equipment

1.   What is the front of the saddle called?

2.   What do you call the short whip that is carried while riding?

3.   Name three of the natural aids.

4.   What is the back of the saddle called?

5.   What is the name for a bridle that has a single bit with a curb chain and both a curb and snaffle rein?

6.   A martingale controls movement of which part of a horse?

7.   What is the near side?

8. The saddle and stirrups were invented about what year?

9. A crib strap prevents the swallowing of what?

10. Why would you put a neck cradle on a horse?

11. What is the off side of a horse?

12. Tony Lama boots come from where in Texas?

13. What are stirrup coverings called?

14. Where do you put a horse's hobbles?

15. Where do you put a twitch?

16. Egg-butt and twisted wire are terms used to describe what training equipment?

17. True or False: The thinner the mouthpiece, the more severe the bit.

18. What is the jaquima?

19. A wide band placed around the horse's barrel behind the withers with rings attached to accommodate reins is called what?

Equipment — Questions

20. Why do western bits have mouthpieces that curve?

21. What is the carved wood that strengthens and shapes the saddle under the leather called?

22. A bridle with both a snaffle and a curb bit is called a _____.

23. True or False: The bit should go under the tongue.

24. The gullet of the saddle comes above what part of the horse's body?

25. What was probably the first piece of tack used by man?

26. What piece of equipment was *last* to be invented: the stirrup, the horseshoe or the bit?

27. In 1858, what improved piece of equipment did General George B. McClellan introduce to the US Cavalry?

28. Why are holes punched in the bottom of feedbags?

29. What is the duga?

30. In the Russian troika the two outside

horses gallop. What does the center horse do?

31. What part of equipment do these words refer to: sweetwater, mullen and spade?

32. Why do you put a jowl wrap on your horse?

33. What kind of a bit is a Dee bit?

34. What is the advantage of a copper mouthpiece on a bit?

35. What do peacock stirrups do?

36. The A.H.S.A. has ruled that junior riders in hunting and jumping classes must wear helmets approved by what organization?

37. What is a voltage girth used for?

38. Where do you attach the lunge line to a cavesson?

39. What are these terms used to describe: Bavarian gare, brush oxer, Helsinki gate and Amsterdam bank?

40. The English harness consists of a collar around the neck. Where is the Hungarian harness?

41. What do these words refer to: Phaeton, Landau, Char-a-banc and Sylphide?

42. What part of your foot touches the stirrup iron: ball, instep or heel?

43. The western saddle was designed about two hundred years ago. Where?

44. What were Roman hipposandals?

45. Who first invented the stuffed saddle, complete with girth: the Greeks, the Scythians or the Etruscans?

46. What improvement did the ancient Celts make to the snaffle bit?

47. What is a chin strap made of?

48. Why would you put Vicks in a horse's nose?

49. How do you "address your reins"?

50. What is the bight of the reins?

51. Where should the western rein hand be: in your stomach, above the saddle horn, or in front of the horn?

52. Metal loops on the saddle used for attaching breastplate, cinch strap and girth piece are called _____.

53. Smooth wooden poles about three inches in diameter are used to ride over when schooling horses. What are these called?

54. What is another name for the English noseband?

55. What is the belly-band of the saddle called?

56. What piece of equipment on the saddle was invented by the Huns of Mongolia in the fourth century A.D.?

57. What is a "cricket" on a bit?

58. What is the standard-size arena for a dressage contest?

59. Where is a gall likely to occur?

60. Why do bareback equitation riders use hairspray on their mounts?

61. What is an in-hand class?

62. How do horses prefer to ride in a trailer: facing forward or backward?

63. What do you call the leather strap used to fasten the end of the cinch to the saddle?

64. What piece of equipment do these words

refer to: standing, running, bib, Irish, pulley and Market Harborough?

65. What piece of equipment do these words refer to: Flash, Grakle, Kineton and Puckle?

66. As a rule of thumb, cavalletti should be placed how many feet apart?

67. On which side do you dismount, your right or left?

68. Why do you run the stirrup irons up the inside of the stirrup leather after dismounting?

69. The billet guard should be pulled down over the _____.

70. Before mounting you can estimate stirrup length by placing fingertips on the stirrup bar and lengthening the leather until the stirrup iron has touched _____.

71. What piece of English equipment prevents opening of the mouth to evade the bit?

72. What are bell boots made of?

73. What injury do bell boots prevent?

74. What does the sheet protect the horse from?

75.   When do horses wear rugs?

76.   Why would a trainer use a snaffle *with keys* as a first bit?

77.   Why are mutton withers undesirable?

Answers

1. The pommel

2. Crop or bat

3. Hands, legs, back, voice, weight

4. The cantle

5. Pelham

6. The head and neck

7. The side from which you mount or the left side

8. 300 A.D.

Equipment—Answers

9. Air

10. To stop him from tearing at bandages, blankets or injuries

11. The right side

12. El Paso

13. Tapaderos

14. On his legs

15. On the upper lip

16. Snaffle bits

17. True

18. The hackamore

19. Surcingle

20. To relieve pressure on the tongue

21. Saddle tree

22. double bridle or Weymouth

23. False

24. The withers

25. Some form of bridle

Equipment—Answers

26. The stirrup

27. The McClellan saddle, a newer, light-weight one patented in 1865

28. So water can drain out if the horse decides to drink

29. A high wooden hoop which connects the shafts over the top of the horse's body in a Russian harness

30. It trots.

31. Western bits

32. To reduce the size of the throat latch area

33. Snaffle

34. It increases saliva flow so horses' mouths don't become dry and insensitive.

35. They have a safety ring that disengages under pressure from inside.

36. U.S.P.C. or Pony Club

37. Vaulting on and off the horse in gymnastic exercises

38. On the ring on the nosepiece

Equipment—Answers

39. Horse jumps

40. Around the breast

41. Horse-pulled carriages

42. Ball

43. California

44. Leather "shoes" fastened to a horse's hooves; later, iron was used.

45. The Scythians

46. The addition of a chain that fit into the chin groove

47. Leather or leather and chain

48. To disguise his detection of odors

49. You release them and pick them up correctly.

50. The loose ends

51. Above the horn

52. D rings

53. Cavalletti

54. Cavesson

55. The girth

56. Stirrups

57. A roller attached to the port for the horse to play with

58. 20 x 40 or 20 x 60 meters

59. Under the saddle or girth

60. To keep them from sliding around on the horse

61. One where the horse is led rather than ridden, like halter, showmanship, etc.

62. Facing backward

63. Latigo

64. Martingales

65. Nosebands

66. Three to four

67. Left

68. So the irons won't flap against the horse's sides and frighten him

Equipment—Answers

69.   girth buckle

70.   your armpit

71.   Dropped noseband or cavesson

72.   Rubber

73.   They prevent the heels of the forefeet from being hit by the toes of the hind feet.

74.   Flies, insects and dust

75.   Prior to competition or during cool traveling conditions

76.   As the horse plays with the keys he bends at the poll and relaxes his jaw.

77.   Because they make it difficult for the saddle to stay put

Racing

1. What three races comprise the American Triple Crown?

2. What son of Man O' War won the Triple Crown in 1937?

3. Who was the first horse in the world to earn over a million dollars on the track?

4. Both Man O' War and Native Dancer had the same enormous stride. How many feet did it measure at top speed?

5. What son of Man O' War was first to win the Maryland Cup steeplechase three times?

6. What are the two gaits in harness racing?

7. What great sire was the father of Man O' War?

8. What gelding was affectionately known as "Old Bones" or the "Galloping Hatrack" by racetrack fans?

9. Who was the only horse to finish a race in front of Man O' War?

10. Who was the first pacer to cover a mile in two minutes?

11. In 1909, what innovation did jockey Tod Sloan come up with?

12. Who was "Big Red"?

13. How many mares a year was Man O' War allowed to service?

14. Who was the 1978 Triple Crown winner?

15. What is it called when faster horses are given more weight to carry in order to equalize a race?

16. What name is given to the rider of a racehorse?

17. What famous race sire was the father of the great Native Dancer?

18. How long is a furlong?

19. What did Richard Nicholls, the British governor of New York, construct on Long Island in the 1600s?

20. What century does it appear that turf records began being recorded?

21. What is quarter pathing?

22. In what country did steeplechasing begin?

23. Who was the first filly to win the Kentucky Derby?

24. The modern age of racing was ushered in by the "father of the British turf" in 1660. Who was he?

25. Where was the first quarter-mile racetrack in Kentucky?

26. What famous Texan owned the first great "native" American race horse, Copper-bottom?

27. Who wrote *The Matriarchy of the American Turf*?

28. Where is the Kentucky Derby held?

29. What filly which had never beaten colts before won the Kentucky Derby in 1980?

30. Who won the Kentucky Derby in 1985, finishing third fastest ever in the Derby records?

31. Penny Cheney was owner of what Triple Crown winner?

32. Who was the only horse ever to beat two American Triple Crown winners?

33. Who has trained more winners than any other North American trainer?

34. Who won the 200th English Derby at Epsom?

35. What great Argentinian trainer had a particularly successful hand with fillies in France and the US?

36. Who was the first racing filly ever to be sold for $1 million?

37. Who was the only horse to ever win the Ascot Gold Cup three times?

38. What famous racehorse was born during an eclipse of the sun?

39. Where is the English Derby Run?

40. What sire of Dahlia is the great grandson of Hyperion and one of the most successful contemporary race sires?

41. Who was the first American Triple Crown winner, in 1919?

42. Which American Triple Crown winner was named for a city in Washington state?

43. Which American Triple Crown winner also sired a Triple Crown winner?

44. What famous Kentucky Farm owned both the Triple Crown winner in 1930 and the Triple Crown winner in 1935?

45. Which two American Triple Crown winners are named after cities in America?

46. From 1949 to 1973, how many American Triple Crown winners were there?

47. True or False: Man O' War won the Triple Crown.

48. In 1977 Steve Cauthen was named Athlete of the Year by *Sports Illustrated*. What was his occupation?

49. Galant Fox, a Triple Crown winner, didn't even place in one of his races because he was so fascinated in looking at an object. What was it?

50. What famous race track course is laid out around a lake populated with flamingoes?

51.   Where is the Preakness Stakes held?

52.   What are the silks to a jockey?

53.   What famous son of Eclipse was named a strange variation of the word potato, misspelled?

54.   What country is the undisputed leader of breeding steeplechasers?

55.   What is the name of the great steeplechaser who won the Grand National in 1973, 1974, and 1977 (at age twelve)?

56.   Who won the American Triple Crown in 1973?

57.   Where is Belmont Park?

58.   What is the most notorious jump in the Grand National Steeplechase at Aintree?

59.   What is the name of the largest trotting stud in the world?

60.   What flower is traditionally given to the winner of a horse race?

61.   Who sired two of the most sought-after stallions in the history of racing, Nijinsky and Lyphard?

62.   What three races compose the English Triple Crown?

63.   What Triple Crown winner was the turf's first multimillionaire?

64.   What horse challenged Affirmed in his final race, "The Race of the Century"?

65.   On September 12, 1970, the English Triple Crown was won for the first time in thirty-five years by what horse?

66.   Who did Willie Shoemaker call the greatest horse he had ever ridden?

67.   What form of horse racing is discussed at length in the *Iliad*?

68.   What kind of chariot races did the Emperor Nero introduce?

69.   In what year did Secretariat retire?

70.   Name this 100-mile-a-day ride that goes over the Sierra Nevadas. It was named after a president of the Wells Fargo Company.

71.   What does riding "acey-deucey" mean?

72.   A horse in a race having the shortest odds offered against it is called the _____.

73. What is a tie for first, second or third place called in racing?

74. What is a "stayer"?

75. What outrageously behaved sire was the father of Bold Ruler and Nashua?

76. True or False: White thoroughbreds are extremely rare.

77. What disease caused Bold Ruler's death?

78. What is pinhooking?

79. What horse closely challenged Affirmed all through his career to the Triple Crown, coming in second in each of the three races?

80. Where must owners register the colors and patterns of the silks their jockeys will wear?

81. The devil's red and blue silks are the colors of what famous US breeding farm?

82. What famous mare with a flower's name was inducted into the Racing Hall of Fame in 1981?

83. True or False: Citation proved to be an even greater success as a sire than as a racehorse.

84. Who won both the Derby and the Preakness in 1981?

85. What race is called "the Run for the Roses"?

86. What filly won the Kentucky Derby in 1980, coming in second in both the Belmont and the Preakness?

87. True or False: The first winner ever of the Belmont Stakes was a filly.

88. What two fillies have won the Kentucky Derby?

89. True or False: Secretariat (1973) won the Derby in less time than Affirmed (1978).

90. What year did fillies win both the Derby and the Preakness?

91. What famous American race have all these fillies won: Flocarine (1903), Whimsical (1906), Rhine Maiden (1915) and Nellie Morse (1924)?

92. Who was riding the Kentucky Derby winner in 1974, 1976 and 1985?

93. What influential thoroughbred sire is nicknamed "Gray Ghost" or "Dancer"?

94. What horse was awarded Racing's Horse of the Year from 1960 to 1964?

95. Who has the difficult and controversial job of assigning handicaps?

96. True or False: In most foreign countries geldings are barred from classic races and find little opportunity to race.

97. How are post positions determined?

98. Most major race tracks are how long?

99. Where is the Hipodromo De Las Americas?

100. What is a bullring track?

101. What do these terms refer to; outer rim front, jar calk, mud calk and block heel sticker?

102. What courageous filly only lost one race, a match against Foolish Pleasure, where she received a compound fracture which caused her to be put down afterwards?

103. What is the richest source of information for the handicapper, containing all official statistics?

104. Who said, "There is a wide gambling streak in nearly every American man and

woman, a fat streak, fat as a prize hog's bacon"?

105. Where is Exhibition Park Racetrack?

106. Who won the 1986 Belmont?

107. What jockey rode the Belmont winner in 1982, 1983 and 1984?

108. Nasrullah was imported from _____.

109. Longchamps is the home of the classic French horserace called Le Prix de _____.

110. Where is the world's greatest steeplechase held?

111. Where is the Randwick Racecourse?

112. Who was the winner of the first Grand National Steeplechase?

113. What horse with a Hawaiian name won the Kentucky Derby and the Preakness Stakes in 1966?

114. In 1965 the first American-bred, American-owned, American-ridden horse won the English Grand National Steeplechase at Aintree. His name?

115. What horse still holds the record, set in 1973, for one and a half miles at 2:24?

116. What trainer had saddled five consecutive Belmont Stakes winners from 1982 to 1986?

117. What race is the oldest: the Kentucky Derby, the Preakness or the Belmont?

Answers

1. The Derby, the Preakness and the Belmont

2. War Admiral

3. Citation

4. Twenty-five feet

5. Blockade

6. The trot and the pace

7. Fair Play

8. Exterminator

9.   Upset, in the Sanford Stakes

10.   Dan Patch

11.   The monkey crouch

12.   Man O' War

13.   Only twenty-five

14.   Affirmed

15.   A handicap

16.   Jockey

17.   Discovery

18.   One-eighth of a mile, or 220 yards

19.   The first formal racing oval

20.   The twelfth century, in England

21.   Short match races between two horses

22.   England

23.   Regret

24.   Charles II

25.   Lexington, in 1780

26.   Sam Houston

27.   Mrs. Marguerite Farlee Bayliss

28.   Churchill Downs in Louisville, Kentucky

29.   Genuine Risk

30.   Spend a Buck

31.   Secretariat

32.   Exceller (Seattle Slew and Affirmed)

33.   Charles Whittingham

34.   Troy

35.   Angel Penna

36.   Waya

37.   Sangaro

38.   Eclipse

39.   At Epsom

40.   Vaguely Noble

41.   Sir Barton

42.   Seattle Slew

43.   Galant Fox

44.   Claiborne Farm

45.   Seattle Slew and Omaha

46.   None

47.   False

48.   Jockey

49.   An airplane

50.   Hieleah Park in Florida

51.   In Pimlico, Maryland

52.   The clothes he wears in a race

53.   Pot-8-os

54.   Ireland

55.   Red Rum

56.   Secretariat

57.   In New York

58.   Beecher's Brook, named after Captain Becher, winner of the first steeplechase in 1836 at Aintree

59. Hanover Shoe Farm in Pennsylvania

60. Roses

61. Northern Dancer

62. The Two Thousand Guineas, the Derby and the St. Leger

63. Affirmed

64. Spectacular Bid, who lost

65. Nijinsky

66. Forego

67. Chariot racing

68. Races for ten-horsed chariots

69. 1973

70. The Tevis Cup

71. One stirrup leather is longer than the other so the jockey can keep balance on right turns.

72. favorite

73. A dead heat

74. A horse with lots of stamina; one that doesn't give up

75. Nasrullah

76. True

77. Cancer

78. Buying horses as weanlings or yearlings and conditioning them over the winter to resell as yearlings or two-year-olds in training

79. Alydar

80. Jockey Club

81. Calumet

82. Dahlia

83. False

84. Pleasant Colony

85. The Kentucky Derby

86. Genuine Risk

87. True (Ruthless in 1967)

88. Regret (1915) and Genuine Risk (1980)

89. True

90. 1915 (Regret and Rhine Maiden)

91. The Preakness

92. A. Cordero, Jr.

93. Native Dancer

94. Kelso

95. The racing secretary

96. True

97. A volunteer randomly draws numbers to decide.

98. One mile

99. Mexico

100. One with five or six furlongs where the horses are always going around turns

101. Types of horseshoes that racehorses wear

102. Ruffian

103. The *Daily Racing Form*

104. Will Rogers

105. Vancouver, B.C., Canada

106. Danzig Connection

107. L. Pincay, Jr.

108. Ireland

109. L'Arc de Triomphe

110. Aintree

111. Sydney, Australia

112. Lottery

113. Kauai King

114. Jay Trump

115. Secretariat

116. Woody Stephens

117. The Belmont, first run in 1867

Photographs

An exciting rodeo event begins.

1. What event is depicted in the above photograph?

2. What color is the horse in the photograph?

3. What will the rider do with the rope he holds in his mouth?

4. What is the horse wearing around its chest?

5. What famous rodeo in central Washington is held every Labor Day Weekend?

115

Joseph G. Kennedy

The author at fourteen on her favorite stallion.

6. What style of riding equipment is being used here?

7. What type of bit is apparently being used?

8. What white markings does the horse have?

9. What is wrong with the rider's shoes?

10. This Arab stallion sired Been Charmed, a National Champion Hunter. His name begins like the author's. What is it?

116

Having fun at the county fair.

11. What breed of horse is closest to the camera?

12. What breed of horse is being ridden on the inside?

13. What kind of class could these girls be riding in?

14. What riding style is illustrated?

15. What kind of bridles are the horses both wearing?

16. What required piece of apparel is missing from both contestants?

117

Photographs—Questions

The judge gives directions to a 4-H member.

17. What is this required 4-H in-hand class called?

18. What is being judged?

19. What type of apparel is the contestant wearing?

20. What is the horse wearing?

21. If the rider were dressed in hunt seat clothing, what would the horse be wearing?

22. What directions will the judge most likely give to the girl?

Pimlico Race Course

Horses making history on a famous racetrack.

23. What famous American race is depicted in this photo?

24. What was this race named after?

25. Where is this track located?

26. How long is this track?

27. How old are the horses racing in this event?

119

The winner of the Preakness, 1987, in the winner's circle.

Pimlico Race Course

28. What horse is in the photo?

29. What other famous race did this horse win in 1987?

30. What race did this horse lose in 1987 that .prevented him from achieving the American Triple Crown?

31. What is the man on the ladder doing in the background?

32. Who is riding this winner?

Kinetic Corporation

Horses round the bend at a famous U.S. racetrack.

33.   What is the name of this famous racetrack?

34.   What state is this track in?

35.   What famous race is held there yearly?

36.   What is the name of this turn?

37.   What was special about this famous race in the year 1974?

Star Runner clears a jump.

38. What kind of competition is shown in the above photo?

39. What is the striped pole on the ground called?

40. What is the name of the equipment that secures the jump poles?

41. What is incorrect about the competitor's headgear?

42. This horse is an unregistered Appaloosa. When he was born he could not be registered because he had no spots. Is it necessary for today's Appaloosas to have spots?

43. What is the word used to describe unregistered horses?

Chinookum Bars steps onto an obstacle.

44. What obstacle is the horse walking onto?

45. This horse and rider are pictured competing in a class. What is the name of the class?

46. What is the name of the headstall being used?

47. What piece is missing from the headstall that is seen on most bridles?

48. What is the strap called that goes across the horse's chest?

49. Where does the hold down strap attach to underneath the horse?

123

Riskie Affair, the 1983 Canadian National Champion Futurity Mare.

50. What breed is this mare?

51. Identify the numbered body parts in this picture.

Joel E. Clark

Alyson Clark competes on Sea Drift.

52. What style of attire is the rider wearing?

53. What kind of a bridle is the horse wearing?

54. Name the bits in the horse's mouth.

55. Is the horse wearing a caveson?

56. What kind of class is the rider competing in?

57. What piece of equipment is missing that would be necessary for a pleasure class competition?

58. What is the name of this horse's famous sire? Hint: He is an Arabian imported from England by Dr. Howard F. Kale in 1962.

Liz and Lily take a break between classes.

59.   What breed of horse is shown in the photo above?

60.   Where is the registry for this breed located?

61.   The ancestors of this horse must be one of which three breeds?

62.   This horse's color pattern is the most common one. What is it called?

63.   What is the specific name of the snaffle bit being used?

Robin Williams competes at the National Appaloosa horse show in Albuquerque.

64. This purebred Appaloosa is named Make Mine a Double. What term would breeders use to describe his color pattern?

65. If this were an equitation class, where should the rider's rein hand be?

66. Where are rider's numbers usually worn?

67. What is the shiny, oval, silver medal on the bridle called?

68. True or False: It is desirable for the horse to carry his head in a position that is vertical to the ground.

69. True or False: This rider is probably left-handed.

Answers

1. Calf roping

2. Palomino

3. Tie it around the calf's legs

4. A breastcollar

5. The Ellensburg Rodeo

6. English or hunt seat

7. Snaffle

8. Four white sox and a snip

9. They have no heel.

Photographs—Answers

10. Benna

11. Arabian (a purebred named Sea Drift)

12. Appaloosa (a purebred named Chinookum Bars)

13. Matched Pairs or Working Pairs

14. Saddleseat English Style

15. Weymouth or double bridles

16. A necktie

17. Showmanship

18. Cleanliness and appearance of horse and handler, and ability to maneuver horse

19. Western

20. A halter and lead

21. A bridle

22. Turn and trot to the rail, halt, turn, walk back to line and set up.

23. The Preakness

24. The famous Dinner Party Stakes winner, Preakness

25.   Pimlico Race Course in Maryland

26.   1$\frac{3}{16}$ miles

27.   Three years

28.   Alysheba

29.   The Kentucky Derby

30.   The Belmont

31.   He is painting the colors of the winning owner's silks on the weathervane atop the cupola.

32.   Chris McCarron

33.   Churchill Downs

34.   Kentucky

35.   The Kentucky Derby

36.   Clubhouse Turn

37.   The 100th Derby was run.

38.   Jumpting or hunting competition

39.   Cavaletti or ground pole

40.   Jump cups

Photographs—Answers

41. She is not wearing a harness. (None was required then.)

42. No

43. Grade horses

44. The bridge obstacle

45. Trail Riding

46. One-ear or slide-ear headstall

47. The throat latch

48. Breast strap or breast collar

49. The girth

50. Arabian

51.
    1. Poll
    2. Crest
    3. Withers
    4. Croup
    5. Flank
    6. Stifle
    7. Gaskin
    8. Hock
    9. Coronet
    10. Pastern
    11. Fetlock
    12. Cannon
    13. Knee
    14. Elbow
    15. Throat Latch
    16. Muzzle

52. Saddleseat English attire

53. Double bridle

Photographs—Answers

54. Curb and a snaffle or bridoon

55. Yes

56. Bareback equitation or saddleseat bareback equitation

57. The saddle

58. Silver Drift

59. Paint

60. Ft. Worth, Texas

61. Quarter Horse, Thoroughbred or Paint

62. Tobiano

63. Eggbutt snaffle

64. Leopard

65. Above the horn

66. On the rider's back

67. A concho

68. True

69. True

Miscellaneous

1. The first people to bring horses into North America were _____ .

2. What ruler of England decreed that all stallions, except ponies, under fifteen hands should be destroyed?

3. A gray horse is born what color?

4. What is a bay horse with an even sprinkling of white in his coat called?

5. Fifty-five million years ago a horse ancestor left its remains in fossils. What was he called?

6. A foal's size will double in the first how many months?

7. A black horse with an even sprinkling of white in his coat is called what?

8. What do you get when you cross a jack stallion with a mare?

9. A hitch of horses is made of what three sections?

10. A strawberry roan would be what color without his white hairs?

11. What percentage of growth occurs in a horse in the first year of life?

12. What magazine calls itself, "Since 1936, The World's Leading Horse Publication"?

13. What is the purpose of tapaderos?

14. Outcrossing two animals results in a vigorous strong, healthy offspring. This phenomenon is called _____.

15. True or False: Horses that have long backs are desirable.

16. Why would you add linseed meal, cottonseed meal, or soybean meal to your horse's grain?

17. True or False: Horses should have straight shoulders.

18. What is the best roughage a horse can get?

19. Who wrote *The Black Stallion Returns*?

20. What use did the Plains Indians make of inner cottonwood bark?

21. What percentage of pregnant mares produce live foals?

22. Gestation for a mare lasts how long?

23. What does a breeder mean by a maiden mare?

24. What does a breeder mean by a barren mare?

25. What is a teaser used to detect?

26. What do you call an unsightly scar or lump that does not impair the performance of an animal?

27. Did the Plains Indians geld their horses?

28. Why do some people hang empty plastic jugs in their horse's stall?

29. What is the single most important nutritional reason that mares fail to conceive?

30. What is a Caslick operation?

31. What is another name for the afterbirth?

32. True or False: Few twin horses survive.

33. How long is the foal's umbilical cord at birth?

34. Foaling usually takes how long?

35. In the normal presentation, what part of the foal is visible first?

36. What part of the horse's large intestine is similar to our appendix?

37. What is a "cast" horse?

38. What is it called when a horse is allowed to travel in a circle while on a rope held by the handler in the center of the circle?

39. What does a horse lose when he sheds out?

40. What does it mean when a mare waxes up?

41. Should the rider's heel be tipped up or down when he is riding equitation?

42. What US general helped to save the Spanish Riding School in WWII?

43. Where is the Spanish Riding School?

44. Where are a horse's feathers?

45. What president was also the first American mule breeder?

46. What is the name of the little Mongolian Wild Horse named after a Russian explorer?

47. What is a zonkey?

48. True or False: The horse has an excellent memory.

49. What is judged in an equitation class?

50. What rodeo sport was practiced by the Thessalonians in the sixth century B.C.?

51. The oldest engraved tablets written on horsemanship were written in 1400 B.C. by a Hittite. What was his name?

52. To what use did they put the first seven horses which the London Company sent to pioneer Jamestown in 1610?

53. Where was the horse breeding industry centered in Ancient Greece?

54. What is "chrome" on a chestnut?

55. Who brought many fine desert stallions into Spain in the third century B.C. during his unsuccessful attempts to invade Carthage?

56. What is between a horse's incisors and his molars?

57. True or False: Most horses are ambidextrous.

58. What fox-hunting accoutrement did Robert Brooke first bring to Maryland in 1650?

59. Pivoting on the forefeet is called a turn on the _____ .

60. True or False: Backing is a not a natural movement for a horse.

61. How many poles are there in Pole Bending?

62. What constraint was first erected in 1710 at the fall line of the Savannah and Pee Dee rivers?

63. How many years are horses given to jump the lower-than-standard heights in "green hunter" classes?

64. In a jumper class, is it a fault to kick or buck?

65. What does it mean when a horse gets wrinkles above his nostrils?

66. True or False: In a hunter class the fences are raised higher until a winner is determined.

67. Endurance rides are judged on what two factors?

68. Why do some horses wear red ribbons on their tails?

69. True or False: A cow-hocked horse has his hocks too close together.

70. What is indicated when a horse being ridden switches his tail?

71. How far are endurance horses required to travel in one day?

72. When hauling one horse in a two-horse trailer, the horse should always be loaded onto which side?

73. What organization is credited with first introducing dressage to the United States?

74. In cavalry warfare, which suffered more deaths: horses or soldiers?

75. Which European leader in 1806 created

six national studs, thirty stallion centers and three riding schools in his country?

76. In which war was the Charge of the Light Brigade?

77. How many million horses were there in the U.S. when South Carolina seceded from the union in 1860?

78. Upon his death Napoleon's war horse was presented to the Royal United Service Institution. What happened to his hooves?

79. The Bedoins valued their mares as war weapons. Did the Norman conquerors ride mares or stallions?

80. Why did the Mongol armies put slabs of raw beef or mutton underneath their saddles when riding?

81. Which British ruler decreed that all stallions must be stabled and could not run free?

82. The concept of the "balanced seat" was developed by which cavalry school?

83. What did Colonel Alois Podhajsky write in Vienna in 1948?

84. How did a Blackfoot Indian's horse show that he was in mourning for his owner?

85. Ninety percent of all foals are born between 7:00 and 7:00. During the night or day?

86. Why was it difficult for ancient Roman cavalrymen to learn to mount?

87. Mohammed said that for every barleycorn that is given to a horse, Allah will do what?

88. How many ponies did each Mongol soldier own?

89. Which country has about three million horses — the highest of any European country?

90. What is the most difficult level of dressage called?

91. In the travers, is the horse's body bent in or away from the direction it is going?

92. What is the sport of kings?

93. Antoine de Pluvinel wrote a book advocating kindness in training of horses called *L'Instruction du Roi* (1666). Who was his famous pupil?

94. True or False: One feature of many Renaissance statues is that the horses are pacing rather than trotting.

143

95. How many people are on a competition team for acrobatics on horseback?

96. How long is it stipulated that a bronc rider must stay on his mount before the buzzer sounds?

97. The first official jumping competitions were held in 1864. Where?

98. After 1902's International Tournament in Turin, the German emperor forbade any German to participate in further international competitions. Why?

99. True or False: During the war, cavalrymen were issued gas masks for their horses.

100. What color is an albino foal when born?

101. True or False: Horses were among the very first animals to be domesticated.

102. What do these words refer to: Dentzels and Mullers, Parkers and Philadelphia Toboggans, Herschell-Spillmans and Stein and Goldsteins?

103. What color is the hoof below a white stocking?

104. What is a stargazer?

144

105. What rodeo sport uses a jerkline?

106. During what war did the US abolish its horse cavalry?

107. What was the name of the act passed in 1934 that resulted in capture and impounding of wild horses?

108. Polo came to England from what country in 1869?

109. What mail system in 1860 depended upon relay riders at fifteen to twenty-five mile intervals?

110. The connestoga wagon was named after a city in what state, where it was made?

111. What happened when Achilles scolded his horse?

112. Pope Gregory III forebade the eating of what?

113. What Roman emperor made his friends dine with his favorite horses?

114. Who owned Crabbet Park Arabian Stud?

115. What color are the mounties' horses?

116. Who brought fifteen or sixteen horses to Mexico in 1519?

117. What is the emblem of Mongolia?

118. How did Muybridge in 1872 find out how a horse trots?

119. In 1873 three troops of fifty men each formed to administer justice and peace to Saskatchewan and other vast regions. What was this group to become?

120. What was erected by the Chinese to protect their northern frontier from plundering Hsiung-nu horsemen?

121. True or False: Horses were despised by the Hebrews and are mentioned infrequently in the Old Testament.

122. What Greek cavalry officer wrote two books in 430 B.C. to lay the foundations of classical equitation?

123. What three different tests comprise the three-day event?

124. True or False: Show jumping is a sport where men and women compete on equal terms.

125. Polo is played in sessions of seven and a half minutes called _____.

126. In Baz-Kiri Mongolian riders try to get a

carcass from each other across a goal. What animal is sacrificed?

127. Where does the scent of a fox come from?

128. True or False: Halter horses have the insides of their ears shaved.

129. Why would a horse have a donkey tied to his halter lead?

130. What does it mean if a horse has black points?

131. True or False: Most horses can be ridden when they are one and a half years old.

132. When turning a horse you are leading in a circle, do you push the horse toward or away from you?

133. Who stands "under the spreading chestnut tree"?

134. What book says, "Blessing, good fortune, and a rich booty shall be attached to the forelock of horses until the day of the resurrection"?

135. If wishes were horses, who would ride?

136. What famous poet wrote a poem about stopping his horse by the woods on a snowy evening?

137.   The movie *A Man Called Horse* featured which Indian tribe?

138.   What was the only western to win an Oscar for Best Film (1931)?

139.   What off-beat western shows hero John Wayne getting killed?

140.   What is the proper way to hang a horseshoe for good luck?

141.   What Greek "peace offering" foiled the defenses of the Trojans?

142.   What god of the sea is said to have invented horse racing and the bridle, and is said to have fathered three horses, including Pegasus?

143.   Where is the Kentucky Horse Park, the $27 million facility that houses the International Museum of the Horse?

144.   What artist's earliest and most famous of his Western Series of sculptures is entitled *The Bronco Buster*?

145.   What sport does the French Societe d'Encouragement oversee?

146.   An early engraving of two wild horses found in Switzerland dates to the Early

Stone Age (1,000,000–50,000 B.C.). It is called the Commando Baton. What is it carved into?

147. What famous rodeo in Alberta, Canada, is called a "Stampede"?

148. "After God," said the Spanish conquistadores, "we owed the victory to the _____."

149. Cortez left Spain with sixteen horses. How many of them were stallions?

150. In classes over jumps the rider first rides in a circle. What does the rider do last?

151. True or False: Jumpers are judged on performance, manners and way of going.

152. The stride of an average-size horse is about _____ feet.

Answers

1.   Spanish conquistadors

2.   Henry VIII

3.   Black or brown

4.   Red roan

5.   *Eohippus* or *hyracotherium*

6.   Three

7.   A blue roan

8.   A mule

9.   The lead, the wheel and the swing horses

10. Chestnut or sorrel

11. 80 percent

12. *Western Horseman*

13. To protect the boots and keep the feet warm

14. hybrid vigor

15. False

16. For added protein

17. False

18. Good pasture

19. Walter Farley

20. Supplemental feed for their horses

21. 60 percent

22. 337 days, or 11 months

23. One that has never had a foal

24. One that produced a foal previously but did not foal last season or is not in foal at the end of the breeding season

25. Mares in heat

26. Blemish

27. Yes

28. To give the horse something to play with when bored

29. Obesity

30. Suturing the upper vagina shut

31. Placenta

32. True

33. Two to forty inches

34. Fifteen to thirty minutes

35. The front feet and muzzle

36. Caecum

37. One that is stuck down next to a fence or wall and cannot get up

38. Longeing or lunging

39. His hair

40. She will soon foal. (She gets wax on her teats.)

41.   Down

42.   General George Patton

43.   Vienna, Austria

44.   On his fetlocks

45.   George Washington

46.   Przewalski's Horse

47.   The result of a zebra-donkey match

48.   True

49.   The rider's abilities

50.   Bull-dogging

51.   Kikkulus

52.   They were eaten.

53.   Thessaly

54.   White markings

55.   Hannibal

56.   An empty space called the bars

57.   False

58.   A pack of hounds

59.   forehand

60.   True

61.   Six

62.   The first cow pen

63.   Two

64.   No

65.   He is angry.

66.   False

67.   Time and condition of horse

68.   Because they kick

69.   True

70.   Discomfort or irritation

71.   50 or 100 miles

72.   The driver's side

73.   The United States Cavalry

74.   Horse losses were about one-third greater.

75. Napoleon

76. The Crimean War, at Balaclava

77. Six

78. They were made into snuff boxes.

79. Stallions

80. To make the meat easier to chew

81. Henry VII

82. Ft. Riley's

83. *The Spanish Riding School*

84. The mane and tail were cut short.

85. Night

86. Stirrups had not been invented yet

87. Pardon one sin

88. Twenty

89. Poland

90. Grand Prix

91. In

92. Horse racing

93. Louis XIII

94. True

95. Eight competitors, one substitute and a trainer

96. Twenty seconds

97. Ireland

98. Because the German riders performed so badly

99. True

100. White

101. False: wolves, sheep, goats and llamas were.

102. Carousel horses

103. White

104. A horse that carries his head too high

105. Roping

106. WWII

Miscellaneous—Answers

107. The Taylor Grazing Act

108. India

109. The Pony Express

110. Pennsylvania

111. His horse foretold Achilles' death.

112. Horseflesh

113. Caligula

114. Lady Wentworth

115. Brown or black

116. Hernando Cortez

117. A horseman galloping into the rising sun

118. He took consecutive pictures of moving animals in rapid succession.

119. The Royal Canadian Mounted Police

120. The Great Wall of China

121. True

122. Xenophon

123. Dressage, Speed and Endurance, and Show jumping

124. True

125. chukkas

126. A goat

127. Glands under the tail and from the pads

128. True

129. To teach the horse to lead

130. It has a black nose and lower legs.

131. False

132. Away from you

133. The village smithy (the blacksmith)

134. The Koran

135. Beggars

136. Robert Frost

137. Sioux

138. *Cimarron*

139. *The Cowboys*

140. The open end should be up, otherwise the luck runs out.

141. The Trojan Horse

142. Poseidon

143. Lexington, Kentucky

144. Frederic Remington

145. Racing

146. A reindeer horn

147. The Calgary Stampede

148. horses

149. Eleven

150. Rides in another circle

151. False: hunters are.

152. Twelve to thirteen